THE
HUMBLE HERO

LIAM ZOLLO

For more on Liam Zollo, go to
www.liamzollo.com

For more information visit www.liamzollo.com

DEDICATION PAGE

TO MY FAMILY

Foreword by Shaun Kenny Dowall and James Tamou

Shaun Kenny Dowall, NRL premiership winner 2013 and New Zealand Representative

I first met Bunno, AKA Liam Zollo, 12 years ago when I moved from NZ and enrolled in the Clovelly Crocodiles Rugby League. Liam and I immediately shared common goals and interests, and 12 years later our friendship is as strong as ever.

Liam has experienced many things his life. He uses his life experiences and giving nature to help and inspire people to live their lives to the fullest potential. His "never give up" attitude and work ethic has allowed Liam to achieve some amazing goals and be successful in life. I think if everyone took a page out of Liam's book, the world would be a better place.

Liam is passionate about helping people and has the motivation and experience to accelerate achievements.

These achievements include running a marathon with only 27 days' preparation; winning an amateur boxing fight; as well as Liam and I breaking a Guinness World Record together (with only hours of preparation). Liam talks about becoming an accelerated achiever, which caters to our generation of instant gratification.

Before he became an accelerated achiever, he had to learn the art of becoming a Humble Hero which helped him to honour his word, be disciplined and to always show up. Liam never stopped no matter what bullies or negative people in his life who told him "he couldn't do it".

From these principles, we could all benefit and become Humble Heroes to overcome adversity and build character to achieve our own goals in a Humble way.

James Tamou, NRL premiership winner North Queensland Cowboys 2015, NSW representative and Australian Rugby League representative

I met Liam Zollo when we were both picked for Sydney Roosters under 20's side. I was immediately drawn to him because of his positive outlook in life and calm demeanour. His family was nothing but welcoming, and to this day we remain close friends.

I believe this book will help others to conquer their fears and be inspired.

He is always there to share his wisdom around business and success. An example of this is when we were launching our new business with my beautiful wife Brittney. Liam spoke on the phone and was excited about the possibilities and helped us start. Because of this Tamou fitness is going great and you can find us all over the country.

I believe through Liam's story of The Humble Hero it will help others to face adversity, conquer their fears and be inspired.

Contents

Introduction

Immediately reading the title of this book you may think it's about me, but if I were to claim I'm a hero, it would be hypocritical to the title itself. This is actually a book about the people who have helped me to achieve success.

I refer to mentors who saw something in me that I didn't see in myself. Those mentors are the HUMBLE HEROES who guided me to recognise and understand what it means to be successful in all areas of life, through being humble whilst also in the process of learning about life.

Everyone should become aware and accepting that we sometimes need to go through times of adversity, perhaps even bullying, and ultimately let go, in order to find personal growth and success in life.

It's learning how to tap into and access those real-life heroes that can prevent you from living a lifetime of chaos and pain.

It's encouraging you to take those opportunities to stop, listen and learn from those who have walked the path before you.

It's recognising and understanding that even though there can be momentary and often intense pain, this is part of personal growth and overcoming life obstacles, there are HUMBLE HEROES all around to help us step up to enjoy life in its entirety.

You can be a HUMBLE HERO too.

Why would you need to be a hero and humble to be successful?

A vast majority of people who search for success often think they have to outdo others in order to reach it. They think that they need to dominate their competition and be better than them in order to succeed, sometimes at the expense of others.

This isn't true.

We can be a hero and humble simultaneously.

Genuinely successful people don't feel the need to be egotistical or seek praise, recognition and status from others in order to acknowledge their own success. They are often the givers - the sharers of wisdom and knowledge. They seek out to give praise rather than searching to receive it.

HUMBLE HEROES are ultimately those that us humble humans often aspire to be more like.

In being a HUMBLE HERO it can be useful to look at people in the world who make a big difference through humility. For example, are we more likely to positively remember Malcolm X, a man with a vision and purpose to help others? Or Donald Trump, a man with a vision and purpose to help himself?

All of us have the ability to step up and be the hero in our life. By modelling everyday heroes like our parents who feed us, clothed us, give us money. As well as the teachers that guide us, the grandparents and relatives that care for us, the community that supports us and those people who come into our life when we need it most.

Being a HUMBLE HERO is about recognising the people that helped you to get into the position you are in now. It's about seeing those experiences, positive or negative, and learning from them, whilst using these lessons to guide and help others or even to increase your own success.

It's about being grateful for the people who set you

challenges to complete (that you sometimes don't want to do) and realising that you do have support; it may just come from unlikely areas.

The silent hero

An important step to being a HUMBLE HERO is becoming a SILENT HERO.

By following rituals that real-life heroes use everyday, we are able to consistently evolve as successful humble beings. You don't have to step on other people's toes to get what you want. You also don't have to brag about yourself in order for people to notice the difference you make in the world.

I've learnt some of the most successful tools and ideas of living which I share with you throughout this book, including examples from the negative times in my life, which will assist you in your own life's successes.

The SILENT HEROES are the ones who don't call themselves heroes. All the mums, dads, brothers, sisters, teachers, coaches, friends, and neighbours. The people who lift you up when you're feeling down. It may even be the ones you thought pulled you down when really they saw something more in you that you didn't see in yourself. They were simply urging you to dust yourself off and pick yourself up. The ones who understand that evolution, personal growth and helping the next generation is the key to successful living. The ones who stick around when others don't have the capacity to stick it out. Even the unlikely heroes that you may never meet, who are designed to help you get to where you are now and help you become a HUMBLE HERO in the future.

You may think you're not successful, but you already are. You're alive. You're breathing. You've done a whole lot of life learning already. It's now time to be humble enough to pass your success - your growth through both failings and achievements - onto others, without bragging or telling anyone how good you are. If you have to tell everyone how good you are, you are still seeking external validation rather than valuing yourself. Being humble is about recognising and thanking others who have made and will make you stronger and more successful in life.

This is how you become a HUMBLE HERO.

How to use this book

The idea of this book is to read the chapters and let yourself be drawn to the principles that you can relate to most and being guided by insights that might help you to achieve results in your life right now.

This isn't a formula for the answers, rather the strategies to help you achieve your own successful stories and life experiences. One, several or even all of the principles in this book can guide you; all you have to do is pick the one that you can relate to and one that you believe will help on your journey to success whilst remaining humble.

One

Mastering the art of achievement

Mastering the art of achievement is valuable to anyone, because success is the sum of the achievements you accomplish.

It doesn't matter what achievement you are striving to accomplish in life, the most important thing is to see it through until the end. You have to follow through with both a plan and action based on that goal. Only then will you be able to measure your journey and success.

Nothing else should come into your mind to distract you from this goal. Thank you Napoleon Hill, who taught me this in his legendary book *'Think and Grow Rich.'*

When I was **25 years old,** breaking a world record was the only thing I had in my mind. Nothing came in to my head, apart from gathering hundreds of people into one single significant boxing event. I had no previous experience on breaking a world record; in fact the largest fitness class I had ever conducted was just 50 people. On paper this world record was difficult to achieve.

I had so many things to consider - including lack of life experience - but I knew I had to stick it with it until the end if I was going to succeed.

I've made it a life mission to set myself specific high performing achievements and see them through, even when the end feels like it may never arrive.

Running a marathon

I accomplished running a marathon in the 2015 Sydney Running Festival with only 28 days of training and minimal running experience.

Whilst this was a massive feat, I was able to achieve it because I didn't overload myself with other massive goals at the same time.

If I had tried training for an event such as a marathon, whilst also trying to break the world record for the largest boxing class and starting my personal training business at the same time, it would have been a recipe for disaster.

I would have had an abundance of head noise saying all sorts of things that wouldn't have supported my plan to complete my goal through to the end. "See, I told you, you couldn't do it." "Don't worry about marathon training tonight." "Don't worry about the world record." "It's hard mastering a world record and running a personal training business, let's just sit on the couch instead of doing anything." "I have too much going on."

Thoughts like these will continue unless you put a stop to them. Saturation will lead to procrastination. People don't realise that once you bite off more than you can chew, it promotes anxiety and stress to fulfil more tasks.

See tasks through to the end

Some of these examples are big goals with massive feats, but it's also important to look at the small achievements. Every achievement leads you to a place of fulfilment. These accomplished achievements drive you to create more fulfilled achievements.

The more you tell yourself you are going to do something and you accomplish it, the more confident you will become in life overall.

I urge you to start small and gain confidence in setting goals and achieving them. The more you achieve the more successful you become. The more successful you become, the greater life experience you will have.

It's important to set a task and achieve it, learning new skills, which help you build the self-awareness that you can do anything that is important to you if you put your mind to it and take action.

The biggest lesson about following through with your goal or your achievement is what you learn. Even if you feel like you are going to fail, push through anyway. The more you follow through with something, the better you get at sticking to your word and sticking with a plan.

Don't hop from task to task, while never really achieving anything. Don't start something new before you finish the other task. Become a master of achievements by seeing things through to completion.

Back to running that marathon

When I ran the marathon in 28 days, I knew I hadn't done enough. Prior to the event, people were laughing at me for undertaking this training in just 28 days.

I remember being 36km into the race and stopping due to a hamstring injury. I kept going purely because I said I would finish this marathon. Not out of ego and not to prove people wrong, but purely to follow through with a plan I said I would accomplish.

First of all, I silenced the people who told me I couldn't do it. But that wasn't the main thing I learned from accomplishing this goal. I found a new respect for people who train for multiple marathons. Through stretching myself and seeing my goal through to the end, I gained profound respect for a new avenue of fitness, as well as gaining new skills and lessons to share with my personal training clients.

Through completing that marathon I have a new skill to fast track an endurance sport. All of this learning goes into a toolbox I can use in other areas of life. The focus is not to brag about my achievements but simply to help others reach their fullest potential through sharing some of the life learning experiences I have gained.

T H A N K   Y O U

Thank you to the random policemen who gave me a kick up the butt to keep going when I stopped running at the 36km mark.

Tips

- Finish a task that you set yourself;
- Enlist people to encourage you to follow through with this task;
- Don't pick a task that is your strongest asset, test yourself on something you're typically weak at doing and see what you learn by stretching yourself.

"Success makes or breaks you, don't let it define you, let it guide you."

A Humble Hero

Two

Use failure as a trigger

Sometimes achievements don't work out.

When I was 26 years old I decided to complete the first challenge to help Sydney "tighten your waistline" and reduce the obesity epidemic that is plaguing our beautiful city.

I gathered 50 people and together they lost 500cm for Sydney. This event was a success.

The next event was not.

One year later I was provided with a great learning curve. I went from success to mess because of one new element I introduced to the mix – the inflated ego, which I gained from the previous event.

I had decided to take it to another level and gather 500 people for the next challenge. I thought everything was scalable. I thought if I could do 50 I could do 500.

I hired Facebook marketing gurus to take control of the Facebook page. I changed the name and put more money into it with less elbow grease. I injected less passion and drive into it, thinking I could just piggyback off the previous event's success, but this mindset became my biggest failure.

I ended up having 16 people in the challenge, less than 1/3 of my original successful event, and a mere fraction of my goal for the latest event.

I became overconfident and arrogant in focusing on this task and telling myself, "I've done it before, it will just happen for me next time."

I quickly realised that I needed to put in 10 times the effort and action if I wanted to exceed 50 and reach 500 people in this new fitness challenge.

It's pretty obvious from the outside looking in where I went wrong. That's why it's so important to be humble and realise that every new experience is different. You have to go into it with the student mentality to learn what needs to be done in order to get the task done. Not every situation is the same.

Yet I couldn't have physically learned that lesson until I went through a failure.

After this experience I learned that it's important to make my choices clear and be aware not to fall into a position of procrastination. Now when I want to achieve goals, I find it important to put a date that is specific to a year, month, day and even time. This applies a little pressure and gives you a cut off time. This is what drives you to the finish line.

The road to sobriety

After travelling through Central America I decided to give up the booze for a couple of months. Not because I had a problem, just because I wanted to detox.

I asked one of my best mates from primary school Kurt, who is one of my footy buddies, a funny man and the life of the party; to write a contract, which involved some bad deeds if I broke it.

I won't go into the details of the contract, but let's just say it involves hot sauce, money, and something I wasn't prepared to do if I broke the contract.

Kurt wrote up a contract and set a start and end date for me to stop drinking. It also stated that if I didn't accomplish the task, I had to give him an agreed amount of money and put myself through all sorts of pain that didn't make drinking worth it.

I announced this on social media and showed the world my contract. I had people who I hadn't seen in years approach me and say, "I better not catch you drinking otherwise I'm telling Kurt. He gets a big pay day from you."

I know for some it might sit a little uneasy to make a contract up to be alcohol free for a few months, but Australia has a high drinking culture. To make an impact and send a positive message out about not drinking, I created a game that everyone could be a part of. I enlisted everyone I knew to be my support in their own unique way.

I succeeded in this task, especially after making a best man speech at an engagement party, where I recited a poem I had written.

I was sober. It was daunting reading out a poem at a party in front of 150 people who were a mixture of wealthy eastern suburbs friends and blokey bloke Australian larrikins that wouldn't take a poem from my mouth too kindly. But I wanted to push myself and help people hear true emotion, humility and shock. Liam Zollo (the man who could barely string an intelligent sentence together) could now WOW an audience with his words, minus the alcohol (because I'd signed a contract to say I couldn't drink to calm the nerves).

This was way outside my comfort zone. But I pushed passed that zone and I did it, thank God no one remembered my poem because *they* were too intoxicated. I, however, enjoyed the experience and being present to remember it.

T H A N K   Y O U

Thanks Kwok and Odie for giving me the space to try my poetic skills (or lack thereof) at your engagement - (thought this may be a bit of humility).

Tips:

- Set yourself a task to achieve. It could be anything from a school assignment, to writing a blog post or a book, or even running a marathon.

- Allocate someone to assist you on your task. A trusted person you can ask for support throughout the journey and to the finish line. Choose someone who won't laugh at you or make fun of your goal and journey, someone who can completely and objectively support you.

- Create a contract to complete your goal. Make it achievable and fun. Include punishment or atonement clauses in the contract and involve the person you have chosen for support to help pick what those clauses may be if you break the contract. Have a bit of fun with it.

- Let them test you and challenge you throughout the journey, much like those inner thoughts will challenge you. Let this be a test for you to step up and prove to those inner negative critics that you can infact do it.

"If there is no enemy within,
the enemy outside cannot hurt
you."

African proverb

Three

Overcoming adversity

My journey towards genuinely understanding how to create achievements only started a couple of years ago. I didn't know I had it in me all along.

I was only 15 years old when I joined the Sydney Roosters (a professional Rugby League club). I was one of the unfit, talentless players selected simply to make up numbers. Well this is what I told myself. Interestingly, this is exactly what I got.

People always got picked over me. It frustrated me because I didn't understand why. I had a great attitude to life and the game. I loved playing Rugby League and I loved being part of the team. But the coaches always gave me the same story, "you're good but others are better."

I read numerous self-help books, listened to motivational tapes and CD's and attended courses from the masters of success. Still, I sat on the bench and didn't get picked to run onto the field with the team.

I kept thinking to myself, even after all this work I'm doing on myself, I'm still a failure.

"Why?" I asked myself over and over again.

Eventually not getting picked frustrated me more. It became a great source of discipline for me to show everyone that I could get a Sydney Roosters jersey on my back, regardless of what people thought.

This team, that I so passionately wanted to make, was only the under 20's side after all. Did it really matter?

Yes.

The Roosters under 20's team wasn't where I would earn the big dollars, even then still I couldn't get there and not getting picked frustrated me more.

Fast-forward two years and I was still in the same position, not getting picked in the same Roosters team. I was negative, depressed, anxious and had others constantly propelling ahead of me.

Determined to succeed

The difference was my unbelievable drive that developed when it came to health and fitness. This was thanks to my dad for constantly taking me to the park to kick the footy around. I went from one of the least fit players in my position to the top six fittest people in the whole club. The top six out of 80 people at the club, and I wasn't even playing in the team!

Fast-forward again another three years.

I actually achieved my goal.

I finally got to place a Roosters jersey on my back for the first time, being provided with the opportunity to play at my favourite stadium.

I thought I had finally made it. I thought I was a hero for being a person that walked off the street into a team with no talent and it would be me that would turn that team around.

Dropping into depression

Unfortunately that high soon faded with the ever-growing competition that was surrounding me. I was immediately dropped two weeks after my proudest moment. Not for my lack of talent but because of the amount of people signed from different countries who were labelled "the next big name."

This spiralled me into depression and doubt. A rollercoaster I struggled to get off.

I thought so low of myself that I entered into a Rugby League team in the lowest standard of competition in New South Wales; the Sydney University 2nd grade team. The majority of people in the team turned up to the game each week hung over and smoked cigarettes at half time.

I had just spent the last five years becoming one of the fittest footy players in NSW, who would do anything to get picked to run onto the field, to now drinking beers before games and topping them up again at half time without thinking of how honourable it was to run on with a team each week.

Little did I know, this low standard of footy would be the very experience that propelled me into my highest Rugby League achievement of playing an International test match for Italy and alongside heroes that I grew up watching.
Even though I went through this rollercoaster period of my life, this experience helped shape so many friendships, and made me reach my highest achievement over the next two-years.

Unfortunately for me, before I reached my highest achievement of playing for Italy, I spent the next 40 out of 52 weeks of that year (post Sydney Roosters and Sydney University teams) injured and bed ridden from a broken collarbone, ankle injuries and a near foot amputation. Honestly, I think that these injuries were a reflection of my mindset at the time, I felt broken - mentally and (of course) physically.

Looking back on this period in my life, I believe it was my negative mindset that led me to put in only 50% effort into my training and diet, which naturally made me weaker and prone to more injuries.

The power of the mind

A focused mental state is so important when things are going wrong. We drop our guard physically and emotionally when our mind is out of balance. We then become prone to more injuries, setbacks, obstacles and ultimately failure when our mind is not clear.

Make peace with your past

I decided I would put on a representative team jersey and make peace with Rugby League, even after five years of such ups and downs and consistently failing at every attempt to better myself. I had what Tony Robbins calls a 'stacking moment' where you say, "That's it, I have had enough of being this way."

Within days of this decision and returning to Rugby League training in the Sydney Universities 2nd Grade side, my coach suggested I try out for the Italian Australian residence team.

I didn't even know the Italians had a rugby side.

I made sure I was at that trial, no matter what.

I ended up making the team that were going to play

Greece, Malta and Portugal in a round robin. I didn't even know these countries played Rugby League and due to injuries from players that were certain starters I was given an opportunity to play. I was put in a position on the wing (not my usual position), which became a defining role for my Rugby League career. I thanked the staff for giving me that opportunity.

Being given the chance to play professionally, in a game I loved, allowed me to gradually regain my confidence in myself as a Rugby League player and a humble hero in the making.

It was such a high for me to represent a higher standard of footy again.

This was soon shot down, once again, four months after a successful campaign, which unfortunately our team lost to Greece in the final of the Mediterranean cup. I was back up and full of confidence after playing for Italy but then when I went for a trial at a different representative team, involving all Universities in NSW, I got dropped from the team all over again. I was slowly learning that it didn't matter what you have achieved in the past, it only matters if you can keep performing right now. I was too reliant on playing for Italy and expected to get into this other team by default.

This repeated story seemed to become the 'story of my life.' One glimpse of success and feeling on top of the world was immediately followed by being dropped and feeling down. This pattern kept repeating itself. I was beginning to learn that I needed to be dropped to propel me to excel in other areas. The thing I needed to learn was to look at what was happening around me. Life wasn't all about making a team and I shouldn't judge myself on things I can't control.

Soon after being dropped from the NSW student's team, I decided to head overseas for a six month long mini retirement, despite the fact I was only in my early twenties. During this time I lost my personal training business, stopped playing footy, and fast tracked to becoming a man driven by alcohol over the next three months (this was not a smart idea!).

While I was travelling throughout Europe I received an unlikely email from the Italian coach Carlo, who wanted me to play a test match against Wales (who were the European champions in Rugby league at the time).

Carlo, the bubbly northern English speaking Italian sent over 1,000 emails to players saying something along the lines of, "Hello gentlemen, we are getting the Italian Rugby League team together to take on Wales." I was excited by this news because this was the biggest game in Italian history. The Italians couldn't even field a team in the past now we had some world-class players putting their hand up to play. This was all preparation to make the first ever world cup in a sport that Australia dominated. However, my problem was with coach Carlo telling me that I had to go to the north of Italy and that it was likely that I wouldn't get picked.

I didn't listen to the coach and decided that I would travel north to play in the local Italian league team. I had my heart and mind set on it.

I headed up north and ended up in this little town outside of Venice, where I was the only English speaking man training hard in order to join the Italian team. My chances of making the team were slim but I had blind faith.

The trial game day finally came along and I was nervous for many reasons; I was picked for the lead role in the team, and in addition to that I was not able to speak a word of Italian. I was wondering how would I communicate with this team when I couldn't even speak the language? But instead of beating myself up I decided to have fun with it. That attitude ended up being the very reason I ended up playing well and getting selected. We ended the trial game on a high and I was picked for the Italian National team to play against Wales at their home ground two weeks later.

It's funny where life can take you. One minute I'm vagabonding throughout Europe, certain I was due to retire from my brief career as a Rugby League player, and the next I'm about to play an International test.

We made it to Wales and were presented in front of a crowd of 3,000 hostile Welsh folk with plenty of healthy banter. The stadium was roaring and I remember warming up with an inner sense of calm, when really I should have been nervous.

Now, I want to mention that International footy was not recognised outside of Australia. I never thought much of it until I was warming up and I realised how much of a great experience it was for me to be picked.

We ended up winning the physical battle against Wales, even though we were expected to be absolutely smashed.

It was then that I finally started to believe in myself, visualised what I wanted and what I always talked about, and made it into reality.

THANK YOU

Thank you to my Dad, Carlo, Jimmy, Benny and all the coaching staff who have helped me and believed in me. You are my heroes for helping me overcome adversity.

Tips

- Do what you love to do - even if it sounds stupid to other people.
- Always put your hand up and say yes to a task that is aligned with a goal that will make you proud.

"There is nothing noble in being superior to your fellow man; true nobility is being superior to your former self."

Ernest Hemmingway

Four

Losing your ego

Guatemala is a place where I really transitioned from an egotistical self-righteous fitness professional, to a person who understands that everything is a learning process. I also learned that I'm not the best at everything. There are others who are better than me at tasks and that's okay.

I learned these valuable life lessons when I was 26 years old travelling throughout the mountains.

The Guatemalan trip came five years after my previous travelling experience, where I travelled throughout Europe, ate nice food, played Rugby League, and did what every other young male was doing at the time - drinking plenty of alcohol. This time I was smarter, stronger and more confident. But I was still full of ego.

Instead of trying to outdo others, I now ask people that are more experienced than me to assist me. I now live with a constant student mindset. I live each day with the wonder of a child learning a new task.

As a result, I now seek out leaders, instead of thinking I always have to be the leader. I allow myself to be lead by others who have travelled that journey or completed that task before. I make achieving my goals a fun process by learning from the best.

In order to learn new skills and attain mastery in new areas, you should enter each new challenge with a student mindset. Instead of assuming you know everything before you have completed the task. Using this mindset I found I am now open to accepting that I might not know everything and these discoveries allow me to become more successful in life.

The climb of my life

When I was travelling through Guatemala, Kurt and I undertook a massive challenge of climbing a mountain with an experienced guide, known as Moi.

I learned a lot about what it means to be a HUMBLE HERO whilst climbing that mountain with Moi leading the charge.

Moi climbs the mountain every day. On the day he took Kurt and I up, he even completed it without water, while I guzzled three litres. Moi was smaller than me in height and width, but there I was drinking water like I hadn't had any in weeks.

I made the assumption that I was better than him because I looked stronger and I played representative Rugby League. "I tackle six foot tall men for a living, I will be able to climb this with my eyes closed" I told myself during that Guatemala climb challenge.

Children leading the charge

Children are a fantastic reason as to why evolution needs to happen in order for the world to progress.

Our world cannot be solved at our same level of thinking, and so we need an outside view and a new level of thinking to solve our current problems.

Children don't have a predisposition of what and how the world is. They look at it differently, with a fresh perspective compared to adults who have been hurt and are conditioned to their current way of living.

Steve Jobs claimed that this is why children are important to develop in life with no pre-disposition on what the world should be like, and create a new way of doing things in order to have a better world.

We have reached this 'taking' mentality, which in itself is a point of view that has been passed down from generations to lead us to a place where we have conquered the world.

Unfortunately, charities exist to stop world hunger and yet there is still hunger. Maybe we need a new way of creating a better world, especially when we have passionate young creative minds that can assist our current level of thinking. Instead of donating to charities perhaps we can teach people to be self-reliant. We give them technology, training and other resources so they can solve their own hunger.

This is the same for depression and anxiety. I have gone through depression and extreme anxiety because that's what my emotions have been taught in the sporting and business world.

Transforming from anxious to calm

Perhaps we need to look at anxiety and depression as low points which need to exist in order to know when and how to feel happy and calm. Then we would be more aware that we aren't people who are depressed or anxious, we are merely having moments of depression and anxiety.

Maybe we could conquer this disease by recognising that every low returns back to its normal and maybe even peak.

Every action has an equal or opposite reaction, every decision is going to either make us better or worse. It doesn't matter, we just have to take action so we can learn and continuously grow. This is a law of physics.

Anxiety is a moment of being outside our comfort zone - it's just that everyone's comfort zone is different.

Someone may feel outside their comfort zone going to the gym, whereas I feel that's completely within my comfort zone. That same person may think surfing is inside their comfort zone, whereas I may think tackling 10-foot waves is beyond my capability.

If you can look at anxiety as a useful tool to push through barriers, to grow and seek resolution, and to feel calm in the future when you do it again, then you can look at overcoming many obstacles in life. We need to feel anxious to get to the point where we feel calm. Staying in the space of feeling anxious and not doing anything about it won't allow us to progress or transform.

I digress on my story. I think if we want to create a new level of thinking to solve our current world problems, we need to allow younger minds to assist with future generations and come from a giving mentality instead of taking. Giving time to educate people, giving food to the homeless, being at service with skills to help other people make a better world. We should give instead of taking all the time.

I am no preacher and have no desire to be; I just think it's our old level of thinking post World War 2 that we are still living in this program that we need to take from the world as a survival mechanism.

We live in an abundant world where anything is possible. We need to share this with future generations and people younger than us, in order to create the platform for them to solve the current problems we have in the world that we cannot.

Back to Guatemala

Now, back to my story on how I lost my ego. Let me share with you my experience as a mountain climber.

My mate and I had no previous experience climbing mountains. All we did was hire a guide to take us to the top. Kurt and I were simply vagabonding through Central America and decided that we should do something active. Kurt is a great physiotherapist and I'm a good trainer so we were a good team.

We decided to climb Acatenango, with a height of 3,976 metres.

We set off at 4:00am to find our guide Moi at the base of the mountain laughing at us. I thought it was a group challenge but when we arrived, little Moi, who stood four feet tall and rugged up for winter just laughed on arrival.

Kurt and I were dressed in board shorts and shoes that we could have worn to a nightclub - not very appropriate climbing gear (now I understand why Moi was laughing at us).

I thought there was going to be some debrief with safety instructions but this wasn't Australia (the place with all the rules). This was Guatemala. No safety precautions, just to follow little Moi, our guide, up the mountain.

Moi couldn't speak English and Kurt and I could barely order a beer in Spanish. My version of Spanish was taking an English word and putting a Spanish sound on it. I remember asking Moi to stop by continuously saying, "El-stop-o."

The first 300 metres up this dormant volcano was so tiring that it felt like I already climbed the 3,976 metres.

I think it was our naivety that was one of the keys that got us through this climb, because if someone told me in hindsight what we were about to do I probably wouldn't have done it.

I think that is a great message for anything we do. Allow yourself to look at life and learn like a kid - naive and being lead by people who do it regularly.

At the time I thought we were unfit trying to keep up with Moi. Every time I tried to pick up my speed, our guide would go faster. This was a continuous seesaw for the whole climb.

When we reached 3,000 metres I remember stopping and feeling sick. I remember saying to Kurt and Moi to go ahead leave me behind, where I also had a moment of meditation.

Kurt would probably disagree and tell everyone I was borderline passed out. I think the latter is probably truer.

I was now far behind Kurt and Moi, but I managed to get myself back up from my meditation/passing out state and regain some energy to complete the journey. I climbed the last 700+ metres like a man on a mission, slowly catching Kurt to the top.

When we reached the peak of this volcano, ironically it was quiet because the voices in my head were so loud.

I gave Kurt a high five and thanked God for making it up there. I was sick, tired, frustrated - and thankful it was over.

I remember some American tourists coming over to us afterwards, cheering us on and saying, "well done on your accomplishment." We didn't know why they were so happy for us. I asked them why they were making such a fuss and cheering us on. They told us how quickly we climbed the mountain and said it was faster than anyone else.

It's funny how internally I felt as though I had failed because I didn't feel I was fit and climbed the mountain poorly. It didn't feel like that Hollywood movie where I got the pretty girl, had the achievement and success with no issues.

Climbing Acatenango was a pure struggle but I would do it again.

That's why I feel it's important to recognise the pain and hardship that you have to go through in order to achieve a goal.

Success can sometimes be hidden

The American tourists told us that we completed the climb to the top in three hours, while they completed it in eight hours and slept on the mountain overnight. We did it in less time than it took for the sun to rise. Wow! I had no idea.

My biggest lesson is that being naive and finishing a task with someone who has done it before without any predispositions will help you see it through to the end.

I would have never climbed this mountain if I had been told how cold, hard, and fatiguing it would be. I would have never turned up at 4:30am that morning to meet Moi if I was told I was going to pass out before even reaching the peak of the mountain.

Sometimes it's important to not have the whole journey planned out, and just go on that journey to discover how much you can achieve if you give yourself the chance to do it.

T H A N K   Y O U

Thank you Kurt and Moi for helping me achieve this. You're truly my heroes in helping me drop my ego.

Tips to drop your Ego

- Show everyone what you have done, not what you intend to do.
- Thank everyone.
- Be a student to everything you intend to do.
- Find people who are better than you at a task that you want to be better at, and enlist them to help you achieve that success.

"The world we've made, as a result of the level of thinking we have done thus far, creates problems we cannot solve at the same level of thinking in which we created them".

Albert Einstein

Five

Always show up

I find it both exciting and challenging to realise that life is a sum of events, or even built on destiny, that are pre-requisites that come back in the future.

Either destiny or randomness, law of attraction or visualisation of what you want sub-consciously; it doesn't matter. Everything that has happened, has happened for a reason; to keep you alive and growing mentally, physically, emotionally and spiritually.

It's ironic how this life journey of mine started with pain, depression, and low self esteem, yet now I look back on it and smile with a sense contentment knowing how it worked out in mine and the villain's favour. That's why I believe that there are no villains - just unlikely heroes that help you in the future.

My journey to becoming a HUMBLE HERO started when I was 15 years old, asking my Rugby League coach if I could train two ages above so I could become a superstar. I soon realised there were already superstars in this age group.

I was quiet, lacking confidence and willing to train hard to get what I wanted. My problem was that the players didn't like that a younger player was allowed to play with them when I wasn't up to their standard.

Some of the players would tell me to stand at the sideline and watch, while the coach told me to go in and have a go. The problem was that the coach would be focusing on other areas of the training, so I would always go and stand on the sideline in the rain and watch everyone else become better.

The moments I did get a chance at charging in and showing my skills were when the players would tell me to go stand on the wing. This was next to the sideline and the people on the wing were barely being used in these scenarios. Even the wingers wouldn't be standing on the wing. My teammates had me out there just to make up numbers.

I felt so much pain from embarrassment, frustration and that feeling of wanting to crawl under a rock and not be seen. But I couldn't crawl under any rock as I was standing directly in front of 30 other guys who witnessed my ultimate embarrassing moment.

I remember there was one player, Frank, who actually turned out to play super league (which is a high standard of rugby League in England). He would always tell me to stand on the wing. I was always heartbroken when they did this and got depressed and down because I felt like I was always being picked on.

Now, I understand I was just a kid and being groomed for my future in life, in health and fitness, but at the time it was hard to take.

The irony of life

Fast forward seven years later when I was travelling through Europe and given the opportunity to play for Italy in Wales.

I remember our Australian-Italian players calling this guy so we could meet him before the game, just to say hello. The boys were pumped, and so was I. I didn't know who they were talking about and they didn't say his name because they were continually side tracked by women stopping us in the street asking us if we were the Italian team.

I don't know why people were so fascinated with us because we weren't the big teams like Australia or New Zealand. We didn't care though; we just liked the attention which made us feel like rock stars.

We met this man who everyone was keen to see and it ended up being Frank, the man who always put me down when I was 15. He was a celebrity around that little town because he played professional Rugby

League in that area and all the boys played with him back in Australia.

I was so upset seeing him again. It brought up a whole lot of pain that I just wanted to knock him out from just looking at him. I suddenly felt insecure around this guy when just 10 minutes earlier I was feeling like a celebrity myself.

How did I go from superstar celeb status to that insecure 15-year-old kid lacking confidence in seconds?

This moment with Frank and others like it teaches me it's important to understand the past is a pivotal moment leading you to your future. I'm learning and accepting of this more and more throughout my journey to become a HUMBLE HERO.

Heroes appear in surprising ways

The night I played against Wales representing Italy,

Frank came to the game to watch us. He sat on the sideline on a cold windy Welsh night, taking it all in.

I took a moment to realise that the one person who always told me to stand on the sideline and watch him train, was now watching me from the sidelines play the highest-level rugby League match I had ever played.

The irony continued when I was playing on the wing that night, because I was playing the exact same position I learned from Frank seven years earlier.

I saw Frank after the game and he was such a humble guy – truly a great man. I was now able to see him for who he really was and what he contributed to my journey of becoming a HUMBLE HERO.

I always had this preconceived notion of Frank being a mean person because of how he treated me in the past. My memory of him was negative as I thought he was a bully and not so humble, not like he was on that cold windy Welsh night.

Learning this life lesson showed me that sometimes people bully you or push you around because of their own insecurities. Sometimes people appear rude but they can actually be nice and decent people. Sometimes they have something to offer beyond what you can see.

T H A N K   Y O U

Thanks Frank for teaching me to show up and for being a role model for me in how to be a HUMBLE HERO. Through my experiences with you, it taught me that I can let go of the past if I go along with the ride that is life, because that may be the very ride that will propel success in the future if you let it.

Tips of Showing Up

- Always go to the top person who can help you achieve success, enrolling them to help you succeed. In my case, it was a Roosters coach who probably didn't believe in my ability but still helped me to fulfil my dream.

- It's ok to be embarrassed and not have all the answers, but always turn up to training or practice regardless, because you never know where it will lead you and what you will learn in the process.

- Thank the people who push your buttons and pick on you, because that pain you feel will be turned into success, if you keep focusing on what you want.

"A great man is always willing to be little".

Ralph Waldo Emerson

Six

Honour your word

Honouring your word is the most powerful tool you can use in order to be successful in life.

It's still a work in progress, but I really do notice more so that when I don't honour my word, I begin feeling bad and that's when negative head-noise creeps in.

I learned the value of honouring your word from a great mentor - Luis. He adopts a self-help, modern day westernised Buddhist mentality to life. He told me, "the degree in which I honour my word, is the degree in which I live my life."

Wow! I love that message, because the more I practise saying it and doing it, the more I am living my life with meaning and purpose.

This is powerful information, because it drives you to live life with more purpose and be more tuned into doing things in life that you really value, giving you meaning and fulfilment.

As a result, more people want to invest in what I'm doing because I am a person who tells, and shows people that I will fulfil the task. In turn, the more people believe in and value the honour of my word.

The obstacle with honouring our word is the level with which we hold it.

Do what you say you're going to do

It's so often that we overload ourselves and start too big, instead of setting a small milestone to accomplish. We tell people we are going to run a marathon, but then fail to complete a small task like doing the dishes or putting out the garbage like we said we would do them.

How are we expected to run 40km, if we aren't practicing honouring our word with the small things?

As I mentioned earlier, success is the sum of our completed achievements. This starts with your word.

Start with small things and build from there. For example, if I say I'm going to be somewhere at 2:00pm to meet a friend, I'm there at 2:00pm - not 2:05, not 2:10, but 2:00pm.

I know it sounds simple, or even obsessive, but the more you practise honouring your word, the better you become at living with honour every day. Practice makes perfect, so start honouring your word and see what you learn in the process.

I always feel better knowing that I'm honouring a task, and it feels good to be living my life with purpose.

Another issue with honouring our word is that we can honour our word in some areas and with some people, but not others. Don't beat yourself up about it, however be aware of what you promise people and yourself.

If you tell yourself you're taking a break from catching up with friends and drinking alcohol for the week, and you end up on an alcohol infused bender over the weekend, then you will put yourself in a position of dishonesty. The inner critic will then set in, along with the negative self-talk. "I knew you couldn't live without alcohol for a week." "I told you that you shouldn't have gone out last night."

Give yourself the opportunity to practice honouring your word and seeing tasks through to completion to see what your inner voice says as a result.

T H A N K   Y O U

Thank you to Luis and my family for all the experiences and life lessons you have given me, and for being my HUMBLE HERO teaching me this valuable message of honouring your word.

Tips to Honouring your word

- Make an agreement every day to accomplish a task for a certain time and don't move from it. For example, you may set an agreement to complete 10 minutes of meditation per day. Ensure that you don't miss the agreement. If you say 10 minutes, you do 10 minutes.

- Each agreement should have a time and date because, once you master a small agreement like mediation or exercising every day, imagine what you can do with your savings account or finding a job you have always wanted.

- Tell a friend who you can trust about your agreement, and enrol them in helping you to accomplish it every day.

"The degree in which you honour your word is the degree in which you live your life."

Luis Córdoba

Seven

Monk mentality

There is a growing trend of people wanting to find their Zen state of mind - to reach true enlightenment - this pure energy force that is all positive and giving to the world.

The Dalai Lama is one of the truest HUMBLE HEROES of this notion. He finds pure happiness in his humility, in his art of giving, and through living in this very simplistic yet profound view of the world.

I learned the art of giving from the workshop I attended with my westernised Buddhist guru, Luis. I went to this workshop because a friend said I "needed it". I disagreed with that friend at the time, and yet now I see it was full of great insights into human behaviour.

Some people don't want to find enlightenment, and just want to fulfil their own goals, believing it's important to remain busy regardless of how much you get done or achieve.

I was like this for some time, and still am sometimes, but essentially I am more aware. I realised that I was being a taker in my life instead of a giver. I was obsessed with taking from people, and I didn't even realise I was doing it.

There wasn't anything wrong with me or with what I was doing, I just found a new way to be happy within myself because I wasn't looking for satisfaction or bragging to people about my accomplishments to get self-satisfaction.

My story for understanding the monk's mentality started by becoming a giver. I wanted to be a giver without the ego of telling people about my good deeds.

I became aware that performing good deeds or random acts of kindness, when other's weren't looking, gave me greater satisfaction in knowing that I had contributed positively to the world and to someone's life without needing recognition or contribution from them as a result.

These deeds are known as being a SILENT MONK. An example of being a silent monk is doing a good deed without anyone else knowing about it.

Sometimes, I would place five dollars in a vending machine and walk away – allowing a random stranger to pick something they wanted; I also tend to pick up rubbish from our environment and throw it in the bin. At times, I would pay for the next person's coffee in a cafe and leave, not looking for the satisfaction or the praise that I used to be addicted too.

I know I seem a bit hypocritical now explaining that I am performing these SILENT MONK actions, however I'm sharing it simply to acknowledge the wisdom I gained.

Small things make a big difference

I remember one event that I will share just to show you the power of a SILENT MONK.

I was studying a Marketing diploma, and was sitting in the school cafe stressing about my last assignment. I decided to go to a vending machine, place ten dollars in and then walk away. I sat back down drinking my coffee and continued to stress. Two girls about 18 years old, who looked like they carried the world on their shoulders, walked into the cafe with a posture and conversation that looked and sounded as though they too were having a stressful time. They were talking about their negative home life and their low finances. One of the girls got up, and walked towards the bathroom, then five minutes later came back to the table. Her body language had completely changed. She looked excited, as if she had won the lottery.

The young girl who was just months out of high school trying to define her purpose and direction in life, told her friend that someone had left ten dollars in the vending machine and that she was now able to eat something that day, as she was struggling with money and couldn't afford to buy food.

This immediately released my stress about my studies and help me realise that I helped someone feel better about their day, when prior to that SILENT MONK gesture she was feeling down.

I realised that by doing one small good deed and witnessing the impact of that deed, I was able to change someone's perception about their day and perhaps even their life.

I watched on and saw the girls excited about eating. Such a basic thing changed their reality.

When you do a SILENT MONK gesture, you may never know how you affected someone else. They may not know it was you who did something good, but what you will learn is the art of self-satisfaction - without the need to have others approve of you because instead you approve yourself.

Understand that giving, whether it be small or big, is key to increasing your self-confidence, positive self-talk and healthy mindset.

I really recommend that you go out into the world and do at least three good deeds for people. Whether it's buying a coffee for a stranger, bringing someone's garbage bins in off the street or placing money in someone's car door so that they go back to their car and walk into a blessing of money. All of it will have a positive impact on the recipient, but the gift you will give to yourself in that the practice of giving is immeasurable.

T H A N K   Y O U

Thank you Jimmy, my Duos Lacuna Boys, my Dad and my loving Mother for helping me understand this giving mindset.

My tips of Giving

- When you feel like the world isn't giving you something, give something positive to the world.
- Place money in a vending machine and walk away.
- Pick up someone's rubbish that they left in the environment.
- Buy the next person's coffee before they walk in and walk away.
- Don't tell anyone about your Silent Monk activities, and see how much your world changes.

"Work hard in silence. Let success make the noise".

UNKNOWN

Eight

The space time continuum

Time management skills are an incredibly valuable tool to have in life.

Unfortunately, we are becoming a generation that possess a short attention span; so living with the integrity of using time management skills is harder for the massive population to grasp.

Time is filled by the space we occupy. Unfortunately, we can only occupy a certain number of hours in our own world. That's why it's important to choose our time wisely.

If we break down our week into hours, we will understand that our life consists of 168 hours a week. If we allow ourselves 68 hours sleep and 40 hours for our career and word, we are left with 60 hours remaining each week that is available for freedom. But what do we do with those hours?

Instead of spending this time researching, completing what we are passionate about and fulfilling dreams, we are often on our iPhones, iPads, iWatches, watching television and taking in content in a complete trance.

This isn't necessarily a bad thing, but if more people were able to recognise that these forms of entertainment develop a trance state of mind, then what's the difference between meditation and checking our phones?

There is actually *no* difference, because both of these allow us to talk to our subconscious mind. The dangerous thing is that we start talking to our subconscious and filling that space and time with thoughts of other people and how successful they are. We do this instead of talking to our subconscious and filling it with incantations and affirmations that help us be more positive and aware of our current state.

We tend to go on Facebook or Instagram and focus on how people look (or appear to look), and start asking questions about why we can't be as good looking or as successful as that friend.

These unnecessary thoughts about others are a complete waste of time, and they devalue your life. It teaches our subconscious to be continually drawn to outcomes that don't help you in life and this will not help you to become successful in life.

If you meditate or enter a form of trance, you can actually talk to your subconscious and start to practise guiding yourself to be successful in many situations and asking for more successful experiences, instead of focusing on other people's success when you're watching them on social media, which doesn't serve a purpose in your life.

If you think of your mind as its own Google search engine, and meditation as a form of accessing the Internet, then you are able to ask yourself whatever you want and give yourself the opportunity to receive it.

Isn't that exciting?

It's also dangerous, because if you ask your subconscious Google, "why am I so fat?" Your search engine will give you an answer. Your thoughts will then begin to wonder, which will be ineffective to your time, impact your presence at that time and subsequently you may miss opportunities that are right in front of you.

All of this random self-conscious, self-critical trance like head-talk prevents us from being present and giving ourselves opportunities for positive experiences in our lives.

Focus your mind

A wondering mind is useful because it provides a sense of creation; just learn to channel your mind towards the things you actually want.

Being present is important because if you steer your attention to the current situation, then you will always learn and have more memories that will serve you in the future.

This is why children are so powerful, because they are generally more conscious beings than adults. Kids have a greater capacity to learn more and do this by simply being present.

Your subconscious doesn't know if it's right or wrong, it will just find an answer to the questions you ask it.

So instead of spending your time on mindless tasks like incessant social media and being jealous or envious of others based on how they appear to live their life, start tapping into your own search engine and ask whatever you want.

If you ask it purpose driven and meaningful questions, you will receive the answers that will serve your life with meaning and growth.

For example: If you ask yourself, "Why don't I have enough time?" Your brain will find a list of all the reasons as to why you don't have enough time. If you asked your (subconscious) search engine, "how can I create more time for that task?" your brain already knows the answer.

You may be sceptical about this notion of time, the subconscious mind and the impact of our thoughts, but if you look at humanity over time from the dawn of mankind to now, we are constantly evolving and finding continuous growth by solving problems with our mind.

What we have to realise is that we already have all of our ancestor's errors and successes inside our subconscious to help us with those problems. You just have to ask more accurate and specific questions to get those useful answers.

The best way to ask yourself better questions is

through asking your subconscious what you want. Whether you actually do this through prayer or meditation doesn't matter as it's the same thing.

The universal message is that going inward to talk to yourself and asking for things is a major influence in receiving what you want.

T H A N K   Y O U

Mum, for helping me become productive and teaching me to see my own light.

Tips to beating the space time continuum

- Go on a 30-day social media detox and see how conscious you become.

- Go on a 30-day ban from newspapers, televisions and phones, to take a break from negative content and see what positivity you will see as a result.

"The higher we are placed, the more humbly we should walk."

Unknown

Nine

Survive or thrive

If you want to understand the human mindset, understand that there are inner conflicts that are continually going on inside of our mind.

There is a caveman mentality, which is centred around survival. This is both protecting you and limiting you from understanding a new level of growth.

We become anxious when pursuing journeys outside our comfort zone, because our survival mechanism tells us not to do it. The survival mechanism is necessary for us to survive in everyday life, such as crossing a road. Our inner voice will tell us to stop and look both ways because we know if we don't, we could get hit by a car.

Whilst this is a useful part of our brain,

unfortunately this side also tells us to fear meeting a person in a dating environment, competing in sport or at school, or anything else that pushes us out of our comfort zone.

Unfortunately, when we listen to this caveman survival voice instead of listening to the 21st century thriving voice, we refrain from stepping up in order to claim something new to propel us into a successful version of ourselves.

Either way, it's not so much about being right or wrong, but more about the survival mechanism mentality which may limit our possibility for personal growth.

Don't limit yourself

If you look at a tree that is planted in a little pot, you can see that the roots are limited to the pot size. If you place the same tree in a field that stretches for miles, it will continuously expand and grow.

Humans are exactly the same, but our own potential and self-expansion through events, experiences and breaking barriers are our hypothetical tree.

We grow with our potential through our mind - trees grow leaves, roots and consciousness in a different way.

The difference with a tree and ourselves as humans, is our level of consciousness. We tell ourselves and even others of their limitations, which places us in a pot like a tree.

What if we told each other, "there are no limitations." This way of thinking would provide endless potential growth.

I find it incredibly important to be around people who don't place you in a "pot", keeping you trimmed and groomed in a way that is small and how they want you to be.

Never stop expanding. Just remember to help others by not placing them in a pot as well. This is how we have conscious expansion. When we encourage people to thrive, they let go of limiting themselves with merely a survival mentality.

T H A N K   Y O U

Howard and Bev

TIPS on practicing EXERCISES TO THRIVE

1. Immediately confront a small fear like asking someone out on a date. You just have to take the first step. Or ask someone for help with that task. Even if you fail, at least you have given yourself the opportunity to expand, grow and potentially thrive.

2. Compliment three people on their ability to expand; areas in their life where they are doing really well and perhaps stretching and growing themselves. Tell these three people your own vision for expansion - and if you don't have a vision just yet, then make talking to them about wanting to create this vision a part of your conversation.

3. Set a goal you believe you can't achieve in 30 days and go ahead and do it anyway. For example, the goal may be something such as running a marathon, swimming an ocean swim, or starting a million-dollar business. The difference between yourself and others who

have done it, is the problems that they have solved to get them to their desired results. People who are successful are some of the world's greatest problem solvers.

"Selflessness is humility, humility and freedom go hand in hand. Only a humble person can be free".

Jeff Wilson

Ten

Take out the garbage

My mind used to be forever racing against the clock and continuously trying to get things done. I was always investing energy into thinking of better ways to do things, whilst always scrambling to get them done and never a clear path in my head.

Feeding your body and mind with excessive alcohol or drugs can prevent you from being present; often resulting in not being able to complete the things you need to do.

We can also have a continuous craving to be busy, yet not really achieve much at all.

If you can relate to any of these examples, then it might be time to take out the trash.

In order to go from good to great, it's useful to

understand the things that are preventing you from getting things done and having a never ending to do list.

I learned this concept of 'good to great' from an author and Leadership Advisor, called Jim.

I learned to stop thinking all the time, filling my mind with ideas and concepts, without actually finishing a task.

I used to have a huge list of unfinished tasks that wouldn't get done, and that filled my mind with more ideas and thoughts. My mind was like a garbage bin, full of rubbish and nothing else to fit inside my head.
What happens when you take out the garbage? You're left with an empty space that you can fill with anything you want in your life.

If you're finding it difficult to learn new things, or notice your attention span is constantly wandering, then it's probably time to take out the garbage that exists in your head. If you empty the space in your head, you leave more space for things that you want to appear in your life.

Speak up to create change

I started taking out the garbage in my mind two years ago when I was living with two of my best mates. My business was in debt, I had unpaid parking fines, I was behind on my car registration, and my mates seemed snappy and acted like they were eager to punch me for no reason. To add fuel to this picture, a girl I was seeing at the time was giving me the cold shoulder. I was due to start a fitness challenge with my business to generate more revenue, and I couldn't seem to enlist any new clients. My life in general seemed to be scrappy and didn't seem to be making sense. There was no clarity to my outlook and nothing was going right.

I decided to sit down, with a coffee, and write down all the things that were causing me to overthink and things that felt like garbage in my life.

Taking the time to address issues

My list:

1. Talk to flatmates and find out why they're annoyed and frustrated see how it can be resolved.
2. Pay parking fines.
3. Pay car registration.
4. Determine how much debt I have in my business and pay it off.

This was only a small list but I decided how I could fix every item on the list and through that I gained some clarity.

I phoned both flatmates and individually asked them why they were snappy and frustrated. They both independently revealed they had been busy with work, feeling stressed and didn't realise they were acting like they wanted to pick a fight with me. They appreciated the call and apologised for the stress it had caused in the house.

Addressing this item on my garbage list allowed me to realise that sometimes people have their own stuff going on, and that they also need to take out their own garbage.

One thing was now checked off the list and as a result, I immediately felt lighter. I didn't feel heavy in the stomach anymore and I started to feel better about myself. I realised that confronting my garbage and sorting it out made my thoughts clearer almost immediately.

I continued to work down the list and paid off fines, and paid 6 months car registration instead of 12 so I could maintain my business budget for my fitness challenge. I phoned the girl I was seeing at the time and she told me she wasn't feeling our relationship any more. That was a smack in the face, but taking action on this task on my garbage list then created the space for her to be honest and both of us were now free to get on with our lives, in order to grow and expand in all areas.

I immediately lost my fear of stepping up and addressing issues with people. I also gained confidence in approaching one task at a time and completing it, even if it was overwhelming.

When my garbage list was empty, I realised I didn't have any thoughts that were limiting my overall goal of building this fitness challenge.

I realised that it was the things lingering on my mind that were stopping me from actually completing this challenge and not the challenge itself.

Every time I thought about buying a flyer or speaking to a web designer, I subconsciously said to myself, "you can't afford the website because you have bills to pay." "you can't confidently call new clients because you can't even ask your mates what's wrong with them."

You see how my garbage list was the thing that was stopping me from my goal?

As soon as I cleared the garbage in my mind, I had time to focus my energy on the things that were important.

I ended up starting a challenge and calling it "Tighten Sydney's Waistline". We had 54 people in a 30-day fitness challenge, and I raised $5,500 worth of revenue in a week for my business. I thank the garbage list for helping me to raise that money, and for helping my clients to achieve their own personal success as well.

When you clear the space in your mind, you create the space to have clarity and direction on the things that matter.

T H A N K   Y O U

To Jase and Charlie for being the best mates and even better flatmates.

Tips on how TO DUMP THE TRASH

1. Write a list of all the things in your life that you need to get done. Everything from clothes washing, doing dishes, paying bills, having that conversation with a friend, family member or colleague that you are fighting with or the need to clear your energy.

2. Review the list. Decide if you need to delete things from the list because they are not really important, or if you need to add anything else to the list. The exercise is to help you gain clarity through confronting the tasks that are limiting your current thought pattern.

3. Pick five of the most important items on the list that are heavy in your life, and confront them no matter how scary it is and do it. Just get them done.

4. Give yourself a timeframe to tick off your entire garbage list, and tackle five new items each time until your list is complete.

"I learnt to identify the false love from true ones by their fruits, humbleness and how free they were from worldly desires".

Santosh Avvannavar

Eleven

Life with the Commandos

When I was working for a Rugby League club, we attended a three-day commando camp. It wasn't the usual commando camp that was about bonding and team building, this was far worse.

They swore at us, abused us physically and mentally, making us do things that I didn't know I could even do, like holding a push up position for over an hour while doing a team drill.

We had to push trailers through national parks with dead trees in the way, even though some of my peers were severely injured, including a mate that broke his ankle. The commandos didn't help either. We had to carry this wounded teammate on our back for 5km because he completely snapped his ankle.

This was definitely the full commando treatment.

I was cursed at and referred to as a certain swear word so many times, that I began believing my own name was that swear word. I was only a staff member of this club and not even a player in the heavy duty training for the footy field, but I still participated.

We slept four hours in two nights. We weren't given the ice bath after training or recovery warm downs like usual athletes were given. We had to keep going, commando style.

I thought it was very dramatic and unnecessary in some parts because the boys' best still wasn't good enough. We came together and fell apart, but still we kept going.

The true life lesson we received from this commando training was at the end. To unwind and complete the program, we had a beer with the commandos, who went from being brutal men, making us train for 48 hours straight, to gentlemen in an instant. They debriefed us on why we were put through so much torture and sleep deprivation. They probed and asked us if we knew why they were so hard on us throughout the entire course.

We thought it was because they liked it but they told us that in order to gain true character and find true growth, we need to overcome adversity and stress.

Wow! That blew my mind away. Why couldn't they have told us that from the start?

I do understand that I need to go through times of pain in order to see success. I realise that the bullying I have received has driven me to stand up for myself and that enough is enough. Sometimes we do need to push through hard and struggling times, because that's where we will often see our greatest growth.

after this experience I now know I can run for hours and not minutes, and can find another push up even though my arms appear dead.

This is why commandos protect us and go to war, because they know that their character has been tested so much, that they shrug off normal workouts that we find so tedious in everyday life.

Adversity can lead to growth

If you are being bullied or know of someone being bullied at work, university, school or in everyday life in general, know this is an opportunity to step up and grow through adversity.

When you are tested to ask someone out on a date, or starting a new business, remember that all of this is an opportunity to build your character.

The more you push through adversity and stress, the more you draw upon experiences from the past that will propel you in the future.

T H A N K   Y O U

To Coach Ben, the Souths Rabbitohs Rugby League Club and the Commandos for giving me the opportunity to learn these incredible insights.

TIPS TO EMBRACE YOUR INNER COMMANDO

1. Always be willing to accept change in all parts of your life.
2. Place yourself in times of stress to practise overcoming stress.
3. If your boss or teacher is a hard arse, then take their abuse but let it pass through you and learn 2 things; your boss is making you better, or take it as an opportunity to be thankful for how much better you will treat people when you have the opportunity to be the boss.

"The only thing that overcomes hard luck is hard work".

Harry Golden

Twelve

The importance of Creation

When we were travelling through Central America, I would continuously notice my friend Kurt on his phone - looking like he was mastering the art of texting his soon to be fiancée. I couldn't understand why he was always texting, especially on a van fit for 10 people, and yet 16 of us were all crammed in for a 14-hour non-stop trip up a mountain.

I used to try and sleep, but Kurt would continue to immerse himself by typing on his phone.

Why?

I decided to approach him about this over a few Cervezas. I wanted to find a way to politely ask him to put his phone down and be present on our trip, but what I found out is that I wasn't the present one.

When I asked him why he was constantly on his phone, he told me he was writing poetry. My initial thought was to hold back the laughter.

He said it was a way for him to pass time, open up a new part of the brain and remember the trip.

Just listening to another person's perspective on life and travelling gave me a completely new view of life itself. I decided this was a great way to pass time on our 14-hour bus ride.

It encouraged me to start writing too. It wasn't something I'd tried before, but something about travelling and exploring encouraged me to also explore myself, through writing.

As I started writing, embarrassment and failure began to surface. But after a while, the quiet picturesque mountain bus ride provided a new source of entertainment.

Remember I came from a butch footy player, win at all costs to beat the competition kind of background, but this new way of sitting and utilising a different mindset actually tapped into a potential in myself I never thought I had.

It was the catalyst I needed to give me the confidence to write, and now here I am one year later writing my first book, sharing my stories and putting them out into the world.

Don't limit your future success by your current abilities

Am I a master writer? Hell no. I have always told myself I was hopeless. Maybe that's because others branded me as hopeless, because I can't provide great grammar and punctuation. I could blame anyone in my life but at the end of it when I was forced to sit down and open up a different part of my mind, I realised that there *can* be a point of creation.

Imagine what you can do when you stop telling yourself you *can't* do something? Imagine if you started to believe in being a problem solver, and working from the biggest gift the universe has given us in our lives - the main principle that physics and the universe represents - the universe is a creator and so everything in this life is pure creation.

I realised that when I stopped drowning out my creative side and accepted that others had different forms of creation, I started to attract people and create events that were unrecognisably moulding me into a positive future. In this instance it was to become a writer.

Am I the creative source of becoming a writer? No. Kurt was actually the brave and creative person that helped me to unlock my potential in a different way.

Maybe I can share this with you. It doesn't have to be poetry or writing. Your artistic and creative side can be found in building, painting, drawing, music and many other forms of art and creative expression.

Sean, who is one of my oldest and best friends, finds creation in being a builder. He always uses the quote, "people paint, people draw, but I found art in the buildings I build."

We so often brand ourselves as methodical machines that can do anything, and yet we limit our own possibilities by creating a boundary that will limit our potential - our very own creation is limiting our creation.

Life is limitless

What if we followed a rule that anything can be created? Life would be limitless. What do you think the possibilities of life would look like?

Endless.

Don't limit your own creativity by telling yourself and others thatyou aren't creative. Work on your own creative skills - explore life and your inner creative side, like a kid again.

Remember that you are unlocking a new skill set, that you may even be able to use later in life. I began writing poetry that improved my writing skills, and that ultimately lead me to writing my first book.

A poem by Liam Zollo

Creation is ubiquitous

There are simply no bounds

Stay focused, ignore all superfluous sounds

Constantly search for the next form of growth

Repeat the mantra, the positive oath.

Creation is the universe, it is right here

It is this blue planet, not far but near.

This vibrant planet, this glorious earth

and all it encompasses, continual birth

Follow the light, set your back to the dark

You can inspire others, you can leave your mark.

T H A N K   Y O U

Thanks Kurt and Seany for teaching me to become
creative.

TIPS TO BE CREATIVE

1. Pick a creative outlet: music, singing, playing an
   instrument, song writing, rapping, drawing,
   painting, building, developing a business idea,
   building a website, writing poetry, writing a
   book. Try something that you tell yourself you
   aren't good at doing.

2. Pick a habit for 2 months that is different and
   spend 20 minutes a day doing it. Even if you're
   stuck it doesn't matter, just do 20 minutes.

3. Do it every day and see what you unlock.

4. If it doesn't work after 2 months, then pick a new
   form.

5. Every time someone tells you they can't do it, don't put them down, bring them up by unlocking their creative source.

"The creative adult is the child who survived".

Unknown

Thirteen

Being fearless

I remember I gained this concept of fearlessness from a coffee catch up I had with good friend and UFC fighter, Richie. Richie is also a part-time big wave surfer, a job I wouldn't have imagined I would like to do part-time.

I asked Richie what it meant to be fearless, and he smiled and told me that he feels fear more than anyone on this earth, especially when stepping into the octagon (fighting ring) or dropping into 30 feet waves.

But he understood how much he faces his fear whenever he gets in the ring. He told me it's like conquering fear every time he faces that thing that scares him the most.

I can relate to this fear when I was stepping into a boxing ring. I was so fearful of being in a fight, to the point where I would say sorry to my sparring partner every time I made contact. When I hit, I would clench tight as if I was preparing for a car accident.

But once I had been hit, I realised that it wasn't as bad as I'd made up in my head. That's the only way to conquer fear and become fearless. It's finding out what you fear the most, and placing yourself in an anxious state to face that fear and conquer it.

Being fearless is recognising fear and being aware of your current state, and yet you still go for it. It's facing the very thing that confronts you and places you in a position of anxiety.

It's important to experience anxiety, because the moment you face it and continue to face it, the anxiety will drop. This is growth and, in essence, one step closer to being fearless.

An example of this is the amateur boxing fight that I was explaining above. The more I sparred, the more I got used to sparring. When my fight approached, my anxiety was replaced by excitement and hunger for the uncertainty. I never knew I had this quality until I conquered my fear of fighting. I was always the person to run far away when anything resembled an altercation. But here I was now, facing the fight.

T H A N K   Y O U

To Richie and my bro John - the men with no fear.

TIPS TO FACING YOUR FEARS

1   Immediately after reading this chapter, face a fear, whether it be small or large, feel the anxiety and push through it.

2   Set up a date with someone, book a marathon,

attend a martial arts session, book a public speaking course - something that will force you to face the fear. The objective is primarily to feel your most anxious state, be aware of it, push through it and see what you learn.

"Only when we are no longer afraid do we begin to live".

Dorothy Thompson

Fourteen

The art of reinvention

New Zealand Rugby League International player Shaun Kenny Dowall is one of my great mates who once gave me some great advice. He said, "To continually succeed, you have to keep reinventing yourself."

Very simple, and yet a slightly scary piece of advice. But I took this on board.

That continually resonates with my willingness to be excited by never being stuck with my current job or working out the same way or relying on the same stories to make people laugh. I continually force myself to do something different.

Shaun, is a professional athlete who has won grand final rings and four nation tournaments with New

Zealand, also helped me to break the first world record in boxing. His ability to put his hand up and try new things is a continuous motivating force for his success.

He meditates with monks, does Tai Chi and yoga, and can also be found practicing the art of being present. He understands that in order to reach new levels, you need to have new levels of thinking.

This is motivating for me, and helps me to drop my ego and know that a big tough Rugby player (as I once thought I was myself) can practise this art of being mindful.

It's never too late to reinvent yourself

If you're at a stage of life where you're feeling down or anxious, it's never too late to reinvent yourself. Remember that until we are on our deathbed, we have a duty to continuously grow through our ability to learn something new all the time.

If we can learn the art of reinvention by understanding the fundamentals of learning a new skill like playing an instrument, practicing mindfulness through yoga, meditation or Tai Chi, or even learning a language, you never know where that skill will take you. The goal you are ultimately aiming for is the art of disciplining yourself and setting an agreement you can stick to every day.

I started learning the guitar because of a couple of songs I always wanted to play, which I still play to this day.

The art of reinvention is humbling to a person - to learn a new skill for themselves without the ego or constant need for reassurance. You're just doing it to have fun and to open yourself up to new possibilities.

Now I go to a party and if I see a guitar I pick it up and play. Immediately people turn around and tell me that they never knew I could play. I love that, because I do it for my own satisfaction. Now I am definitely not a professional and accept that, but I do it because I enjoy it.

Another enlightened moment of reinvention and humbleness came when I moved to Yamba. I closed my personal training business and moved to a town that was full of retired folk. I knew that it I was going to have to find work so I decided to do something different and try the online business world.

Now if you know me, then you will know that I am a 28-year-old man with a computer literary skill set that would represent someone who didn't grow up with technology. In other words, I am not that great at it.

This was one of my greatest challenges. How could I live in a retired town, run a business online as a personal trainer but not actually give people personal training?

It's simple, I started writing programs for footy teams without the need to be there physically. I wrote this book you're reading now, and gathered other fitness trainers' programs together so I can help them sell their programs.

This business is just starting and I have had an amazing response.

Do something or go out and achieve a goal that is for you and no one else. Do something that you need to learn, not necessarily something that you're good at, but something you've always wanted to achieve.

Music and computers never came naturally to me, but I found a way to play guitar and start an online business. Not because I believe I'm naturally skilled (actually the complete opposite) - I accepted that I'm not good at something in order to get myself in a state of being a student again, so I could learn faster.

T H A N K   Y O U

Alison for teaching me to build more online presence.

TIPS TO REINVENTION

1   Every 30 days, enrol yourself into a new course that will reinvent your physical body, through a new weights or cardio exercise or even yoga, Tai Chi or Pilates. It can even be dance, powerlifting or something that is physically demanding.

2   We learn through movement and often remember in pictures not words, so memorising quotes in a book won't help you develop a new skill - you have to move and learn.

"To continually succeed you have to keep reinventing yourself."

Shaun Kenny Dowall

Conclusion

The HUMBLE HERO is a person who doesn't recognise that they are the hero in the story. It's everyone and anyone who understands they are helping people. It's everyone and anyone on this planet.

The previous chapters are common traits that can be found in all HUMBLE HEROES.

HUMBLE HEROES recognise that we are meant to succeed through times of pain and failure, and do this in a positive way that inspires others.

I urge you to do this by stepping up and taking charge of your life, and realising that it's the people we surround ourselves with that define our humbleness and our achievements.

Say yes and follow through with your actions and your word. Remember: your word is your bond. No one should break their bond.

Remember to help others and never criticise or argue with them, because arguments breed arguments, just like success breeds success.

What if we imagined life as a game that isn't set up to win? But more so to find out how you can in the game and redefine the way you play it through your experiences. Remember: everyone has a purpose. Our deep interests and passions drive our purpose, the light inside all of us. We are all part of this one song called the UNI-VERSE.

Remember that there is never a positive or negative moment in our lives. It's our own perception that makes it positive or negative and it's our choice to use these events as ways of redefining or moulding yourself into the person you are today.

Remember, it's your choice whether you see bullies, aggressors and villains in your life as people who caused your failures, or from a point of view that you needed them in your life to test you or shake your current patterns. These people are still needed in your story so you can overcome adversity to build character - just don't let them define your character.

Understand that there is no villain, just your perception that helped you gain self-realisation moments as education to further yourself in the future.

Thank you to all the heroes in my life whom I once thought were villains in my life story, or people that were there for me in my times of need. The simplest things like my dad kicking the footy with me and teaching me loyalty in relationships, my mum for washing my clothes and teaching me to clean. My teammates whom I thought didn't like me but didn't see what I saw. The people who instilled positive habits through acceptance and following through with the goal.

You may have not felt lucky or had lucky experiences but remember, if you choose to find both positive and negative in every situation and see how you can use it to inspire others, your life will have growth and purpose.

I felt unlucky as a child, but I switched my perception as I got older and used these negative experiences and positives to make this book and help me start a new experience on becoming a HUMBLE HERO.

ACKNOWLEDGMENTS

Thank you to:

1. My loving parents for never giving up on me.
2. My brother and his young family for having my back.
3. My loving partner Emily and her family for coming into my life.
4. Coach Ben for teaching me to have ATD ("ATTENTION TO DETAIL").
5. Jim for unlocking my potential in Rugby League.
6. Carlo for teaching me to find the solution instead of the problem.
7. The whole Italian national rugby league community for giving me countless opportunities.
8. The Carpe Cerevisi boys.
9. The Duos Lacuna boys.
10. The ISA family.
11. Jayson and Troy my first fitness role models.
12. Alison and Toni my book coaches.

13. The so-called villains who weren't villains, rather people who taught me to see things differently.

14. Chris - the man who shared my World Record vision.

15. Finally, everyone who I have met who haven't been mentioned, thank you for coming into my life and teaching me something new every day.

About the Author

Liam Zollo started as a personal trainer at 18 years old at Fitness First. He ventured into fitness studio start ups in 2008.

In 2010 he decided to travel overseas to Europe - losing his business but keeping his business skills.

In 2011 he re-started his fitness business and grew it from 0 to 80 group fitness clients in 6 months.

In 2013 he broke the first ever World Record for the Largest Boxing class in the World, and in 2014 Broke the Guinness World Record for the largest amount of people completing "burpees" in 2 minutes.

In 2015 he became an intern at the Souths Sydney Rabitohs as Coaching Assistant, and in 2016 became a rehab specialist with the Souths Rabitohs second division team.

Liam Zollo now lives in Yamba with his loving partner Emily, and concentrates on fulfilling his dream as a Humble Hero.

His dream is to help everyone celebrate their life through health and fitness.